GUIDE TO DEALING WITH OPPOSITE SEX FRIENDSHIPS IN MARRIAGE

Reasons why people ditch their friends when they get married; and how to deal with opposite sex friendship after marriage

Connie Larson

Goodwater Publishing
279 Stoney Lane
Dallas, TX 75212
Texas
USA

CONTENTS

CHAPTER ONE

MARRIAGE AND FRIENDSHIP

Marriage is a formally or legally union of two people recognized by the society. Every culture and religion has various values that are associated with marriage. While in western societies, only two people can become married, other climes permit polygamy, which means marrying more than one spouse. In spite of the type of marriage, marriage is bound together by the care, need, companionship, and values of two people, which can overcome hurt, immaturity and selfishness to form something better than what each person alone can produce. Marriage often starts with a friendship type of relationship. During the first years of the friendship relationship, the couples had spent many evenings hanging out and talking with each other. They shared joys, hurts, and hearts. There was intimacy between the two of them that made them want to get to know one another better and more. They were sure that they had found the love they desired.

Friendship, on the other hand, is a type of relationship in which two people (commonly of the same sex but not always) have similar interests and enjoy spending time together. They support each other when things happen and share the most important events in their lives. It is a deliberate commitment to love another. Unlike other obligations of love, friendship establishes an incredible bond. It is something the two parties enter into knowing that they could keep the commitment, or renounce the responsibility as they have volition and empowerment to leave or at least take space from us one another when necessary. In most cases, our friends do not live with us, and are not financially, legally, or relationally bound to us. Friendship is universal in humanity as it cuts across every stratum of human life. It starts in childhood with the sharing of inquisitiveness, amusement, and toys. As we grow, some friendships develop with us for a lifetime providing companionship, support, and love for each other's beings. The truth is that friendship serves as a mirror of our quintessence throughout our life's journey. The love, amusement, and anxiety we share with friends give us a sense of self which can sometimes be frustrated within our family relations. Our friends become our historians, secret keepers, and fellows in the journey of life.

Marriage and friendship, while they share key areas of overlap, are fundamentally different relationships and can be confused with one another. One way to compare marriage and friendship is to relate to how married couples describe their best friends and how they describe their spouses. Most spouses describe their close friends in terms of positive personal qualities. A good sense of humor, caring, and honesty were the qualities they most frequently evoked, but the range of qualities was broader than the one they offered in descriptions of their spouses. In other words, spouses tend to characterize their partners in terms of roles and close friends in terms of personal and relational qualities. In spite of these better descriptions of friends over spouses, some couples admit that their spouses are their best friends. This is a wrong assertion as calling the person you're married to your best friend may be shorthand for saying that you like your spouse and that you have shared history, shared lives, and shared dreams. But in the end, the expression doesn't do justice to the full meaning of marriage or the whole purpose of friendship. There is an essential distinction between the role of a best friend and the role of a spouse.

There is no denial of the fact that friendship is vital between spouses because both treat each other as if the other is the best friend in the world and most cases, that's what they are. The role of a spouse and a best friend are similar but not the same. This may sound nitpicky, but best friend can never do justice to the far more intimate calling of the marital relationship. This will be minimizing the role of the spouse and aiming too low. The relationship between spouses is so unique, sacred even that there are laws to protect and reward individuals who choose this maximum level of togetherness. The bond between spouses is so highly sought after and gratifying when reached. The marriage vows of "for better or worse" are literal; the commitment that spouses make goes beyond any friendship possible. Marriage is a lifelong commitment. Your spouse should not just know you, accept you, and laugh at your jokes—he or she is obligated to you financially, legally, and personally. No matter how loyal you are to your best friends, you still have separate lives. Marriage comes with a noble purpose, a relationship to protect and nurture, and new responsibilities to contend with together with your spouse.

Marriage opens doors to new relationships. But walking through these doors could mean leaving a lot of things behind. Priorities may change and your life further changes when you have a baby. It begins to revolve around the baby and family. In all these changes, one area that can be affected is our relationship with our friends. Marriage requires you to be in synchronization with your spouse, especially as it concerns your relationships with your old and new friends. Couples often complain about the kind of company their spouses keep and could disapprove of them. This could strain your relationship. Some of the friends continued, especially after marriage could either make or break the union. Even if you don't realize their influence, the links you have with your friends have a direct impact on the quality of your marriage.

CHAPTER TWO

WHY DO PEOPLE SEEM TO LOSE THEIR FRIENDS AFTER MARRIAGE?

There's a general notion that when couples finally get married, they disappear into domestic ecstasy and are never heard from again. But is that really what happens? Does marriage change your relationship with your friends? It's only a little valid, and it's the result of a combination of factors that include a decrease in free time and a shift in priorities. Getting married involves making vows and living up to those vows. It does set off a series of changes—changes that can affect your friendships. This is most true in women than in men because men tend to have few friends than women. Most women especially during singlehood, have a lot of friends mostly co-workers, classmates, neighbors, and acquaintances. They could be besties for such a long time, sharing secrets, going out together, living their best lives, creating memories, and building a memorable friendship out of those moments shared. As soon as they get married, it is not unusual for the married ones to cut off her single friends who have supported them all the while. They start acting like some superior being, as if they just achieved an elevated form of existence, one that places them on a different pedestal of respectability, over and above people who may not feel like doing so in the nearest future or ever at all. A lot of them will tend to forget in a jiffy the years of friendship because of their new status. One begins to wonder if it's the marriage that changes people, or it's just what society expects. Below are some of the reasons why some married people especially women drift from their single friends once they tie the nuptial knot.

Priorities Change

Life indeed takes a new turn once you get married, priorities changes, and so does your life. Major life events, like the birth of a baby, are bound to give us a different perspective on life and make us reconsider what's important and how we'd like to spend our time. People like to think that a relationship with old friends wouldn't change much after marriage, but the truth is that the couples are probably going through a period of adjustment. They are adjusting from being independent and carefree to being responsible and, maybe, respectable; and this can reduce the relevance you have for your single friends. Married people feel their priorities have changed, and they can't relate to the partying-centric lifestyle of their single friends. Some no longer have the high need to socialize because of the time they spend with their spouse, perhaps combined with the interactions they have at work.

Lack of Time

Availability of time is critical to sustaining any relationship, whether marriage or friendship. After marriage and having a baby, making time available for yourself becomes difficult, talk less of meeting or hanging out with old friends, Your spouse takes the time that you could have spent with friends. For some people, in their bid to settle into their new and married lives, they lost contact with their friends as they now have more obligations and responsibilities. It's expected that they have full-time careers and may even have to work extra hours. If they have kids, that's incredibly time-consuming. They will still have to make space to spend quality time with their spouses. All in all, they no longer have tons of spare hours to put themselves out there to hang out with their friends.

Lack of Confidence and trust

Don't be surprised if some of your single friends don't stick around past the wedding day or you decide to cut the off yourself. One of the major causes of such a cut can be the motive of your relationship with such friends before marriage. For example, if your friendship with them was based solely on looking for men together, hanging out late or partying, you may have little basis for the relationship anymore. This is possible if one of the spouses, especially the women, think that those friend(s) may want to take her man from her, or that they are jealous of her. In other cases, due to lack of trust, they will begin to feel that by associating with their single friends after marriage, may drag them into singlehood. Single ladies live a free life, especially the ones that always love partying and hanging out late. Married men or women can't just act that way.

Few things in common

Married people may drift from their single friends after tying the knot because they will cease being similar. They will no longer share anything in common with them because of the change in priorities. Most married people now and then prefer to hang out with other married persons whom they want to hold the same kind of conversations with, for example, they could talk about their husbands, children, or family progresses. On the other hand, if a married person shared this kind of conversation with single friends, they might look at the subject as dull or fail to understand their frustrations.

Change of Location

Moving into a new city, no matter the circumstances, can be tough. Tougher when piled moving on top of a newly established marriage and all the changes that come with it, can quickly become overwhelming. Sometimes couples move to a new city, maybe because one of them got offered a job there. Couples, mainly when occupied with the kids, can find it tough keeping up with old friends while making new ones in the neighborhood. While in the new city, it becomes difficult to always for the couples reach out to their old friends. In such case, the friends may feel that their newly married friend has drifted and so they move on angrily or otherwise.

CHAPTER THREE

FRIENDS THAT WILL BREAK YOUR MARRIAGE

Marriage is a unification of two imperfect persons working towards perfection, leaving out all other parties. This is why wedding vows often include the phrase "forsaking all others." There is no room for a third party in the name of old or best friends to receive an equal share in marriage, because that can easily disrupt the safety of the relationship. With the supposedly best friends present in the marriage, the couple's love gets divided. A part of the couple's heart is taken away from the spouse, where it belongs. For instance, a wife without first letting her husband knows her feelings may tell her best friend how unhappy she is with her husband's behavior. Such situations seldom arise out of bad intentions but betray the trust between the spouses. Triangulation, as such cases are called, is painful and unjust, because the best friend takes what is supposed to be for your spouse. Your spouse never hears from you what you tell others about him or her, and as such, the marriage is run on the best friend's recommendation. Naturally, we all need close friends in whom we can trust and who trusts us, but if that drives us away from our spouse, we certainly stepped over the line. Contrarily, if you find yourself in the situation where a friend relates to you more than his or her spouse, be aware of the dangers of that situation. In spite of your good intentions and willingness to help, you may drive the couple apart if you don't insist that your friend talks to his or her spouse first.

Married couples have different dynamics when it comes to their friends because there is an added measure of checks and balance. Your marriage is the one relationship that should always be your priority. It's common to see that most people don't understand that or perhaps they don't share that same outlook. Therefore, it's imperative to nurture your marriage and ditch friendships that could potentially cause problems. Some types of friends can be a very terrible influence on your marriage, whether or not they are doing it intentionally because we often become like most people we hang out with. While there are loyal and genuine friendships that deserve to be cultivated, there are also toxic friends that we need to avoid. These kinds of friends can cause problems in your marriage, if care is not taken.

The friend who talks badly about his/her or your spouse

This toxic type of friend is constantly bad-mouthing his or her spouse or yours. It's impeccably fine to vent to a friend now and then, but if it becomes a constant topic, then that's when it becomes worrisome. This type of attitude can easily affect your view about your relationship and this can easily influence your behavior. You also need to let your friends realize that it's not okay to call your spouse names or complain about what he or she does or does not do for you. It perpetuates a negative cycle in your mind and thus creates an unhealthy codependent friendship that will harm your marriage.

The stage–five–clinger friend

Stage Five Clinger Friend is a friend that won't give up and is stuck to you like glue. Regardless of what you do, they feel like they want to be around you all the time and can't share you with anyone else. While some friends become more of a family member, it's essential to maintain healthy boundaries still. Which means your friends can't be around you all of the time and you cannot do everything together. You'll find that if you are always including your friend(s) as the third wheel or consistently neglecting your spouse, things may begin to crumble. This brings in divided attention in marriage as your loyalty will tend to be shared between your spouse and stage-five-clinger friend.

The friend who can't keep a secret

Trusting one another is one of the components of a lasting friendship. That's why keeping friends with someone who doesn't value this, who reveals things shared in confidence like it's nothing, is not a good idea. It's not also a good practice to tell too much of your marital problems as this invite unsolicited benevolent, but often biased, advice. This is important when you have a friend who continually breaks your trust by gossiping about you behind your back.

The immoral friend

Friends who don't have the same morals and ethics as you do should be ditched. Moreover, it's good you surround yourself with people that share your views because they're part of the world surrounding you. If you live within negativity, then that's what you will put out. The same outcome is correct when it comes to positivity—if you surround yourself with positive elements, then that is what your result will be. Friends who physically or emotionally abuse their spouses should be cut off as your continually closeness with such friends will tend to influence you negatively.

The instigator friend

This kind of friend often stirs up public feelings especially of discontent or takes pleasure in other's misfortunes. They always find a way to blow small things out of proportion. They can also emotionally intimidate you without even realizing it, focusing too much on how friendship should benefit them more than being a good friend.

The liar

A friend that tells lies with ease is another dangerous friend to have and thus it's important to distance yourself. Unfortunately, there are some people in the world today that receive their happiness by making others miserable. In most cases, these people are very good at convincing you that what they're telling you is the truth when in fact it's the farthest thing from the truth.

The friend who always agrees with you

Yes, you read that right. No real friend will tolerate you all the time, even when you're going down a destructive path. A friend who truly loves you will be honest enough to call you to order when you're jeopardizing your relationship. A good friend should stand out of the crowd and correct you with love and if possible scold you when necessary, all in the bid to bring you out of a destructive path. Keeping the right kind of friends shows how much you value your marriage because you're willing to go out of your way to sacrifice and perhaps cut ties with those who will only harm the happy, healthy marriage you have committed to building.

The friend of the opposite sex

A close friend of the opposite-sex can be dangerous in marriage. It's probably safe to say that we've all, at one time or the other before marriage had a close friend of the opposite sex. Especially where the boundaries are not clear-cut, your spouse may feel threatened by the presence of this opposite sex friend for one reason or another. Always bear in mind; you made a vow to honor your spouse through sickness or in health, so honor it. If you must allow this friend to be part of your life, you'll find that your marriage will always carry a third party that will make things uncomfortable. Make your spouse must feel like your number one.

Friends are an essential, fulfilling part of life, but because they have such a direct influence on our marriages, it's necessary to know who you're spending time with and what kind of impact they are having on you. However, the friends in your life must bring positive elements to the table and must respect the sanctity of your marriage. Communicate with your spouse and make sure that you're on the same page because the reality is if you're friend with someone, then sooner or later, your spouse will also experience those positive or negative influences of your outside friendships.

CHAPTER FOUR

MAINTAINING FRIENDSHIPS AFTER MARRIAGE

A close friend is someone who is always there for you through good and bad times. He or she is someone who listens to and understands you. Someone you can rely on anytime about anything you feel you need to tell or vent. It's someone who will stand up for you in the times when you need it most, keep your secrets close, and someone you can trust with your life. Have you ever asked yourself what live could have being without friends? Of course, boring! Our friends make up part of the closest and greatest allies in our lives, and that shouldn't stop when we get married. Since marriage and friendship are intertwined into one another, let's have a look at some ways in which you can maintain friendships even after you are married.

Show empathy towards your friends

When you get married, it can be hard for your friends (especially if you're the first one in your circle to tie the knot) to admit the ineluctable alterations in your relationships with them. But it's incredible to keep investing the same amount of time and effort into your friendships as before while cultivating intimacy with your new spouse.

You and your spouse need to comprehend that both parties are going to make some adjustments to the amount of time you spend with friends. It's imperative to understand that you're starting a new life together, and spending time together is important. Be compassionate toward one another, and work together to make sure you're meeting one another needs.

It's also important to show empathy toward your friends, who may not understand your need to invest more time into your marriage. If you need to, you can explain to your friends that there have been some changes in your life, and right now you need to honor those changes as you start this new stage of life.

To maintain the friendship, you must try to maintain contacts and make time for your friends. A sporadic phone call or message through internet social media will help you keep in touch with them. A get-together with your friends once in a while would rekindle old friendships. These can help you revive good memories and provide relaxation in the company of your old-time friends.

Create shared friendships

Shared friend or family friend is one of the greatest joys of a healthy and happy couple. There's nothing wrong with each of the couples having individual friends, it's better to make each of your friends a part of your shared life as a married couple. There is a sense of loyalty, and responsibility for friends you've been known through your single years. This helps to maintain a healthy sense of continued connection with them as you transition into this new season of your life.

When couples gather friends together, the spouses get to know the deeper layers of each other in the process, especially if there is a shared past with some of these friends. It's a time to go down memory lane and relive the events of the past.

It's easy to find a single friend you'd like to spend time with, but when it comes to building friendships with other couples, it takes work and carefulness. In spite of that, it's good you expand the social horizon of your marriage by building intentional friendships with other couples who share the same marriage ideologies and interest as you. The mentoring that transpires when you watch another marriage plays out in front of you is a huge bonus.

Maintain individual friendships

Having shared friendships (especially with other couples), doesn't mean any of the couples can't have their individual friends. Keeping connections with old-time friends, helps to enrich the lives of the couples but this entails an open communication with one another about these friends. There is need for the couples to allow one another the necessary space to cultivate these individual friendships.

Sometimes we have a sense of responsibility and ownership for friends who have been loyal to us over the years especially the single years. It's essential to try to pull those friends into your shared life, but there are times when some of the friends you choose might not be your spouse's favorite choices and vice versa.

If your spouse has a friend he or she wants to maintain a connection with, open your arms a little wider to this person. Honor your spouse's shared history with them, and allow your social horizon to expand. Your spouse is loyal to their friends, and it's important to show grace and to respect your spouse's desire to keep this friend in his or her live.

Over time, you may find that the friends who aren't in the center of your shared social circle draw closer to you as a couple. Relationships shift and evolve, and you may find that a friend of your spouse's–who might not have been your top pick at first–turns out to be one of your most loyal friendships.

Protect your marriage from vicious friendships

Sometimes your spouse's friends may not be your top choice (or vice versa), be kind enough to allow them into your life regardless. Shared history is a big deal, should be honored as you get to know your spouse's friends. Sometimes the hardest individuals to build a relationship with at first become your best friends later.

In maintaining friendships in marriage, it's imperative to use wisdom when it comes to integrating past friendships into your marriage. Some of the things to be considered before choosing friends include: Is this friend someone who is disrespectful of you or your spouse? How right is this person? How will this friendship affect you? What effect will this friendship bring into your marriage? Your answers to these questions will determine whether to start, continue or discontinue the friendship.

When you feel uncomfortable with any of your spouse's friendships, approach your spouse to discuss it, be honest, articulate and expressive in your communication. Often, he or she may not have discovered that such friendship is making you feel disheartened. You don't have to seem paranoid or suspicious, but you must open an honest dialog about your fears and doubts regarding the relationship. Be tolerant with your spouse bearing in mind that there may be initial reluctance to change the tone of the friendship or (in most cases) cut it.

Your focus and priority should first be on your marriage. Maintaining friendships that are destructive to your marriage, or that may drift your attention away from your marriage relationship, is counterproductive to this objective.

As you wisely choose to maintain your friendships as a married couple or individually, remember, above all else, to cherish and protect your marriage. You need a solid footing, high confidence, and commitment to ensure a lasting relationship. Build a hedge around your marriage and protect it at all costs, but the truth is that friendship being a positive or negative influence depends on one's character. Secondly, the notion that single friends can be a bad influence on their friend's marriage relationships is false. Just because one is single does not mean he or she has lost direction in life and will bring down your home or drag you back to singlehood. Many married people are worse than the singles out there.

CHAPTER FIVE

CAN MARRIED HAVE FRIENDSHIP WITH THE OPPOSITE-SEX?

Imagine you just got married, and you and your spouse are happily starting your life together. However, you notice your spouse is still communicating with a close friend of the opposite sex that he or she had before you both got married. While you know nothing is going on, you can't help but feel ill at ease. It makes you a little anxious, and you realize you're not comfortable with it. Why is that?

It's a common practice that most married people tend to bring their opposite-sex friendships into their marriage relationship. Such friendships may have been great during singlehood, but bringing it into marriage relationships may be sensitive. Opposite-sex friendships for a married person are risky because such familiarity usually deepens their emotional bonds, and can lead to increased levels of romantic feelings. When a couple marries they make a commitment to one another, a vow of faithfulness, friendship, physical and emotional. This does not mean that old-time friendship must cease, but it does mean that any intimacy shared before marriage must have well-defined boundaries or stop. There must not be any secrets from each spouse, as this can undermine trust, the very foundation of marriages.

Keeping or making friends when married is incredible but, slippery when this friendship is with someone of the opposite sex who is not your spouse. Opposite-sex friendships, no matter how you view it, usually started innocently and later become intense and emotional. You get connected with this friend; realize that you had a lot in common, and before you knew it, you started looking forward to more encounters. In the process, you started comparing your friend with your spouse; you began spending more and more time with this person and even went to lunch a few times. You find yourself sharing more personal details than you had intended during your encounters. Every day you find yourself thinking about this person more and more; before you know it, you realize that you have crossed some significant boundaries. What started as "just friends" had escalated into a full-blown emotional or sexual affair.

NEGATIVE IMPLICATIONS OF OPPOSITE-SEX FRIENDSHIPS ON MARRIAGE

Having a friendship with the opposite sex is not wrong. But it can go wrong for your marriage faster than a wildfire if you are not mindful of your language and behavior. It's not only risky, but it's also a form of betrayal. When a person gets married, he or she is expected to be his or her spouse's lover, confidant, and priority. Here are some of the negative impacts of opposite-sex friendship that may weaken and destroy a marriage:

Risk of infidelity

A lot of married couples have friends that are the same gender as their spouses. It is not uncommon for them to carry old friends into new relationships. However, this can be potentially dangerous to your marriage as it increases the risk of infidelity and relational discontent. While you may be innocent of wrongdoing, your spouse may not appreciate the time you spend with someone else.

Just "friendship" can cross a line

Sexual attractions may not surface until the level of emotional intimacy has progressed to deeper levels. As you come to know and admire someone, feelings of closeness may mature into creating that spark of erotic interest that wasn't there in the beginning. The bottom line is that when you put a man in close, consistent proximity with a woman, very often, feelings beyond friendship will emerge and if you don't have clear guardrails in place, those feelings could take the friendship down the dark path of infidelity.

Lack of time for your spouse

Time is one of the most valuables in relationships. To invest in any relationship, it requires spending your time. When we're investing our time into the building and sustaining of a friendship with the opposite sex, it often means we're taking time away from our spouse. Spending more time on friendships may cause us to start looking for individual emotional needs to be met since probably they are not being met adequately at home. Even when an affair doesn't happen, this mindset can put a subconscious wedge between a husband and wife.

Secrecy

Secrecy in marriage is a show of disloyalty. If there is self-consciousness of not revealing the friendship with the opposite sex or any conversation or meetings with your supposedly friend to your spouse, you have already crossed the line of disloyalty. Lies and disloyalty can destroy trust, the foundation of a marriage.

Feelings of jealousy and insecurity

The power and attraction of the opposite sex friendship make the spouse feel inadequate, jealous, and insecure. He or she might begin to wonder, "What am I not bringing or doing in the marriage? What is wrong with me? Why does my spouse seem so be drawn to this person?" For the sake of marriage, always take your spouse's feelings into account. Sharing unique feelings, dreams, joys, despair, hurts, and trials with the opposite sex friend portray sharing our masculinity and femininity in ways that should be reserved for your spouse alone.

Sharing marriage problems is dangerous

Conversations about marital issues with the opposite-sex friend portray disloyalty and provide a breeding ground for getting needed compassion, comfort, and understanding from a supposedly friend. This is a fertile ground for an affair to spring up because this friend has replaced your spouse as your true confidant in your life.

BOUNDARIES WITH THE OPPOSITE-SEX FRIENDS IN MARRIAGE

Having friends in marriage is healthy and essential to life. Good friends bring a variety of beauty into one's life. However, we must be wise to understand that our friendship with the opposite sex should have boundaries, not just physical, but also emotional. There are no conventional method of setting boundaries with the opposite sex friendship in order to get a secured and lasting relationship. The most important thing is to create boundaries in such a manner as not to create friction in the marriage. The three most important boundaries a married person should have with the opposite sex include but not limited to:

Physical boundaries

For friendship with the opposite sex to strive as a healthy one, the two parties must from onset draw physical boundaries concerning your personal space, privacy, and body. Such things should be saved solely for marriage. Those boundaries which single adults do not have to consider in their relationships with fellow opposite sex singles must be considered in a married person's friendship with the opposite sex. While it's perfectly normal for two single friends to grab lunch, hang out at one's house, or go for a walk. It is not healthy for a married person to do those same activities with a friend of the opposite sex. Don't be alone with a person of the opposite sex outside of work. Romantic relationships come out of recreational activities and intimate conversations. Always have a third party if required to travel or have lunch together. Don't ride in a car or have lunch alone with a friend of the opposite sex as this may create such an atmosphere that leads to infidelity.

Emotional boundaries

Most extramarital affairs do not begin because of physical attraction; they start because of an emotional connection. What may seem like an honest discourse can often lead to an emotional affinity. Couples are meant to create an emotional hedge with friends of the opposite sex. This does not forbid the sharing of sentiments with others, but it does limit what we are willing to share. You should never open up about the state of your marriage, your negative feelings toward your spouse, or specific struggles within the marriage to another person of the opposite sex. When it is necessary to talk to someone; talk to a professional, a clergy, or a friend of the same sex. Do not put yourself at risk of sending the crazy notion of emotional emptiness to someone of the opposite sex. Above all, don't become the shoulder for someone of the opposite sex to cry on. Hand him or her, a tissue and walk away. This doesn't mean that you don't care but it shows that you want to maintain the boundaries in order not to create an emotional attachment.

Time boundaries

For everything there is time, and it won't be out of place to accurately set time boundaries with people of the opposite sex. Single friends can freely call and text one another all hours without restrictions, but this does not apply to married persons. In marriage, the work time should be differentiated from the time you are supposed to attend to your family. Office colleagues and friends, especially of the opposite sex, should not call or text you at odd hours of the day, especially in the night. This does not apply to family members and your spouse. While some circumstances may require a different schedule, keeping general boundaries regarding time is healthy.

Good friends should naturally respect and understand boundaries. If that opposite-sex friend does not recognize that boundary, then view that as a sign that this friendship may not be a healthy one. Even after setting these boundaries, if this friend is very important to you; then make sure that you go out of your way to ensure that your spouse has met this person and is comfortable with him or her. A lot of times, our spouses can discern things that we can't see. Don't immediately label your spouse as insecure if they are uncomfortable with your opposite-sex friend. If you have an opposite-sex friend that your spouse doesn't feel comfortable with, and they have a legitimate reason for their discomfort, then it is best to disconnect yourself from that person. And don't be ridiculous by fighting for that friendship once your spouse waved the red flag. If you value your spouse, then disconnecting from your opposite-sex friend should be easy. If it's not, then you may be implying that you value your friendship more than your spouse, which is a problem!

BALANCING FRIENDSHIP WITH THE OPPOSITE-SEX FRIENDS

Opposite-sex friendships are not threatening marriages unless you or your spouse feels uncomfortable. If your spouse is feeling unnerved by your friendship with a member of the opposite sex; then you need to respect his or her feelings and talk about it or possibly cut it off. Involving your spouse in the friendship may help make him or her more comfortable about your friend, or you could perhaps make the relationship a "couple or shared friendship" with that friend. Go out of your way to show your spouse that his or her needs are most important to you and that you respect your commitment to the marriage.

You don't necessarily have to sever "genuine" friendships with the opposite sex that might be beneficial to you, but you do have a responsibility to find ways to build up your spouse's confidence about your friend. Setting healthy boundaries around these friendships will allow you and your spouse to maintain healthy relationships with opposite-sex friends. You might set boundaries around the settings where you meet and interact with your friend; maybe your spouse feels comfortable with certain settings, but uncomfortable with others. Find out what makes your husband or wife relaxed and comfortable about your friendship, versus what makes him or her nervous and anxious.

Finally, in your friendship with that member of the opposite sex, always be sure to talk about your spouse positively. Display pictures of your spouse in your office where they can be seen, to let people know you're committed to your spouse.

Avoid such places or situations where you might be tempted to omit discussion about your shared life with your spouse, or where you might feel tempted to talk negatively about him or her to a member of the opposite sex. This will set the tone for a safe, healthy friendship.

Made in the USA
Columbia, SC
11 May 2024

35562735R00031